1 CORINTHIANS

Living as Christians

A Guided Discovery for Groups and Individuals

Kevin Perrotta

LOYOLAPRESS.
CHICAGO

LoyolaPress.
3441 N. Ashland Avenue
Chicago, Illinois 60657
(800) 621-1008
www.loyolabooks.org

Nihil Obstat
Reverend John G. Lodge, S.S.L., S.T.D.
Censor Deputatus
June 15, 2003

Imprimatur
Most Reverend Raymond E. Goedert, M.A., S.T.L., J.C.L.
Vicar General
Archdiocese of Chicago
June 24, 2003

The *Nihil Obstat* and *Imprimatur* are official declarations that a book is free of doctrinal and moral error. No implication is contained therein that those who have granted the *Nihil Obstat* and *Imprimatur* agree with the content, opinions, or statements expressed.

To Grace, Louis, and Michel

The Greek text of the quotations from St. John Chrysostom's fourth homily on 1 Corinthians (p. 25) may be found in J.-P. Migne, ed., *Patrologia Graeca,* (Paris, 1862), vol. 61/10: cols. 33–34. Translation by Kevin Perrotta. An English version of the homilies is contained in the Library of Fathers of the Holy Catholic Church, which is available in various printed editions and may be viewed at www.ccel.org/fathers2/NPNF1-12.

The Latin text of St. Anselm's *Proslogium,* chapter 26 (p. 35) may be found at www.uan.it/alim/testi/xi/anselmus_cantuariensis_proslogion_13-26.htm. Translation by Kevin Perrotta. An English translation of the work may be viewed at www.fordham.edu/halsall/source/anselm.html.

The reminiscence of Cardinal Léon Joseph Suenens (p. 65) is taken from his book, *Souvenirs et Espérances* (Paris: Librairie Arthème Fayard, 1991). Translation by Louise Perrotta. The excerpt from the "Dogmatic Constitution on the Church" is from Austin P. Flannery, ed., *Documents of Vatican II* (Grand Rapids, Mich.: Eerdmans , 1975, p. 363.

The Latin text of the comments by St. Thomas Aquinas (p. 75) may be found in S. Thomae Aquinatis, *In Omnes S. Pauli Apostoli Epistolas Commentaria,* vol. 1 (Turin: Libraria Marietti, 1929), 360-70. Translation by Kevin Perrotta. An English translation of Thomas's commentary on 1 Corinthians 13 by Matthew Rzeczkowski, O.P., may be found in Benedict M. Ashley, O.P., *Thomas Aquinas,The Gifts of the Spirit: Selected Spiritual Writings* (Hyde Park, N.Y.: New City Press, 1995), pp. 51–78.

Interior design by Kay Hartmann/Communique Design
Illustration by [name]

ISBN 0-8294-1553-X

Printed in the United States of America
04 05 06 07 08 09 10 Bang 10 9 8 7 6 5 4 3 2 1

Contents

4 *How to Use This Guide*

6 *A Call to Deeper Conversion*

14 **Week 1**
The Foolishness of God
1 Corinthians 1:1–2:5

26 **Week 2**
We Are Taught by the Spirit
1 Corinthians 2:6–3:9, 21–23

36 **Week 3**
Litigation? And Prostitution?
1 Corinthians 6

46 **Week 4**
Do This in Remembrance of Me
1 Corinthians 10:16–17; 11:17–34

56 **Week 5**
The Purpose of Your Gifts
1 Corinthians 12:4–31; 14:1–12

66 **Week 6**
Love Has the Last Word
1 Corinthians 13; Matthew 6:1–4; 18:21–22

76 *Suggestions for Bible Discussion Groups*

79 *Suggestions for Individuals*

80 *Resources*

How to Use This Guide

You might compare the Bible to a national park. The park is so large that you could spend months, even years, getting to know it. But a brief visit, if carefully planned, can be enjoyable and worthwhile. In a few hours you can drive through the park and pull over at a handful of sites. At each stop you can get out of the car, take a short trail through the woods, listen to the wind blowing through the trees, get a feel for the place.

In this booklet we'll drive through a small portion of the Bible, making a half dozen stops along the way, reading six portions of a letter of St. Paul to the Christian community at Corinth. At those points we'll proceed on foot, taking a leisurely walk through the selected passages. After each discussion we'll get back in the car and take the highway to the next stop.

This guide provides everything you need to explore the readings from 1 Corinthians in six discussions—or to do a six-part exploration on your own. The introduction on page 6 will prepare you to get the most out of your reading. The weekly sections provide explanations that highlight what Paul's words mean for us today. Equally important, each section supplies questions that will launch you into fruitful discussion, helping you to both investigate the letter for yourself and to learn from one another. If you're using the booklet by yourself, the questions will spur your personal reflection.

Each discussion is meant to be a *guided discovery.*

Guided. None of us is equipped to read the Bible without help. We read the Bible *for* ourselves but not *by* ourselves. Scripture was written to be understood and applied in the community of faith. So each week "A Guide to the Reading," drawing on the work of both modern biblical scholars and Christian writers of the past, supplies background and explanations. The guide will help you grasp the message of 1 Corinthians. Think of it as a friendly park ranger who points out noteworthy details and explains what you're looking at so you can appreciate things for yourself.

Discovery. The purpose is for *you* to interact with this New Testament letter. "Questions for Careful Reading" is a tool to help you dig into the text and examine it carefully. "Questions for

Application" will help you consider what these words mean for your life here and now. Each week concludes with an "Approach to Prayer" section that helps you respond to God's word. Supplementary "Living Tradition" and "Saints in the Making" sections offer the thoughts and experiences of Christians past and present. By showing what this letter has meant to others, these sections will help you consider what it means for you.

How long are the discussion sessions? We've assumed you will have about an hour and a half when you get together. If you have less time, you'll find that most of the elements can be shortened somewhat.

Is homework necessary? You will get the most out of your discussions if you read the weekly material and prepare your answers to the questions in advance of each meeting. If participants are not able to prepare, have someone read the "Guide to the Reading" sections aloud at the points where they appear. (But notice that the Guide in Week 1 is twice the usual length.)

What about leadership? If you happen to have a world-class biblical scholar in your group, by all means ask him or her to lead the discussions. But in the absence of any professional Scripture scholars, or even accomplished amateur biblical scholars, you can still have a first-class Bible discussion. Choose two or three people to take turns as facilitators and have everyone read "Suggestions for Bible Discussion Groups" (page 76) before beginning.

Does everyone need a guide? a Bible? Everyone in the group will need their own copy of this booklet. The booklet contains the text of the portions of 1 Corinthians that are discussed, so a Bible is not absolutely necessary—but each participant will find it useful to have one. You should have at least one Bible on hand for your discussions. (See page 80 for recommendations.)

How do we get started? Before you begin, take a look at the suggestions for Bible discussion groups (page 76) or individuals (page 79).

A Call to Deeper Conversion

"Now we see in a mirror, dimly, but then we will see face to face. Now I know only in part; then I will know fully, even as I have been fully known" (1 Corinthians 13:12).

Paul's declaration—perhaps more familiar in the old translation "Now we see through a glass, darkly"—marks out the beginning and end of a journey. The point of departure is wherever we are in life today. The destination is the kingdom of God. The journey takes us from our present fragmentary knowledge of God to a vision of God so awesome that we will need to be recreated through resurrection in order to experience it. We travel from shadows toward unimaginable Light.

On such an infinitely long trip, any distance covered is just a start. The deepest conversion is merely a first step, a getting on the road. As we move forward, the Light that is Love makes us aware of the shadows cast by our selfishness and sins. We begin to see where we need to change if we are to reach our goal.

These thoughts about the journey to God bring us to the Christians in Corinth. Some time around the year 50 they heard Paul preach the gospel of Jesus Christ, and they believed it (Acts 18:1–11). From what we can see, their conversion was sincere. They left behind some serious sins (6:9–11—Scripture citations in this book refer to 1 Corinthians except where noted). In fact, they were exhilarated by their new life in Christ. But their excitement did not magically transform their mentality or relationships. Despite the waves of enthusiasm that washed over them, the shoreline of their values and attitudes remained largely unchanged. Indeed, their enthusiasm for Christ soon began to combine with their pre-Christian outlook to yield questionable forms of spirituality.

We do not know how soon Paul noticed problems among his Corinthian converts. After evangelizing in Corinth for some time, he went off to pursue other missionary opportunities (Acts 18:18) but kept in touch with the Corinthians. He wrote them at least one letter that has been lost (5:9). Perhaps in the year 53, or 54, Paul received a letter from the Corinthians containing some questions (7:1) and heard news of them from some mutual acquaintances who had recently been in Corinth (1:11; 5:1; 11:18). He decided to send another letter to his new Christian friends to help them make progress in their journey toward God. Today we call it 1 Corinthians.

In the letter, Paul tells the Corinthians that they are being saved by the gospel they have embraced, so long as they hold on to it and do not believe it "in vain" (15:2). The Greek might also be translated "without due consideration," "in a haphazard manner," "thoughtlessly." This is precisely the issue with the Corinthians. They have accepted Paul's announcement of Jesus' death and resurrection but have not thought through its implications for their lives.

Paul tries to help the Corinthians connect the dots between Jesus and themselves. He leads them back to the basics of their faith, focusing especially on Jesus' final meal with his disciples (11:17–34), his death on a cross (1:17–2:5), and his resurrection (15:1–20). The way that God has saved them—through Jesus' total self-giving—shows that any self-centered approach to life is profoundly misguided. If they will reflect on the roots of their life in Christ, they will better understand how they should live as his followers.

Of course, Paul had instructed the Corinthians in the central events of Jesus' life, death, and resurrection when he first preached the gospel in Corinth. Much of the teaching in his letter, then, is reteaching. In a sense, he helps the Corinthians move forward on the road to God by taking them back to the point where they got on the road in the first place. Retracing one's steps seems a paradoxical way of making progress. But Jesus, crucified and risen, is not only the entrance ramp to the road toward God. Jesus *is* the road to God. The journey to God is the process of coming to know Jesus the Way more deeply and becoming more like him. If the initial departure on the journey toward God is conversion, then progress involves one conversion after another, a returning over and over to Jesus. Every Christian's life is a conversion story—and a story of reconversion.

The Corinthians faced the challenge of outgrowing their self-centeredness and reorienting their lives toward God and toward other people. This is the same challenge we Christians face today. Paul's letter contains a great deal that can help us meet the challenge.

But while, in some ways, the Corinthian Christians were very much like us, in other respects they were different from us, and their society was different from ours. Paul wrote a letter that addressed their particular situation. It is useful for us to get some idea of the distinctive features of the Corinthians' situation in order to understand his message to them. The better we understand what Paul said to the Corinthians, the better we will grasp the message his letter holds for us.

The Corinth of Paul's day was less than a century old—newer than any major city in North America today. We might compare first-century Corinth to nineteenth-century Chicago: a brash, booming city crowded with recently arrived seekers of success. Corinth was a place of dizzying social disparities. A tiny nouveau riche elite occupied the city's socioeconomic summit. Below them, a small group of moderately wealthy people labored ambitiously up the slope. At the base, most of the population, including many slaves, did the hands-on work. The lower class ran the port (Corinth's two harbors made it a major transportation hub), turned out the manufactured goods, and provided the civic and personal services that made life pleasant for the well-to-do. Like city dwellers throughout the Roman Empire, Corinthians in general were intensely status-conscious and unashamedly status-seeking.

Paul made converts up and down Corinth's socioeconomic ladder. While there is no indication that anyone in the Christian community came from the *very* top of society, a few seem to have been major players in business and civic life. Archaeologists have turned up an inscription showing that one Corinthian Christian mentioned by Paul, Erastus, who served as the city treasurer (Romans 16:23), paid from his own funds for the paving of one of the city's streets. But the Christian community was composed largely of poorer, uneducated people (1:26), reflecting the composition of society. Some of the Christians were slaves (7:21).

Belonging to very different social strata, the Christians in Corinth constituted an unusual group by the standards of the day. When the community gathered, aristocrats and slaves, who would not otherwise have related to each other socially, found themselves facing each other across a room and addressing each other as "brother" and "sister" in Christ. Paul tells the Corinthians that the testimony of Christ has been "strengthened," or confirmed, among them (1:6). One way in which the gospel was "confirmed" among them was through its power to draw together people from widely different social levels and walks of life. In status-conscious Corinth, the simple existence of this remarkably varied community of people testified to the truth of the message about Christ.

Paul addresses his letter to "the church of God that is in Corinth" (1:2). The Greek word translated "church" means public assembly. The church was a gathering of people, a community, not a building. There were no church buildings in Corinth, or anywhere else, nor would there be for a long time, given Christianity's lack of legal recognition. Christians assembled where members had homes large enough to accommodate guests. The wealthier members who were in a position to play host to the community's gatherings tended to function as the leaders of the community. One such leader whom Paul mentions is Stephanas (1:16; 16:15–17), probably a wealthy, educated man who had the wherewithal to offer hospitality to the community and do business on its behalf.

How many people belonged to the church in Corinth? While the Christians may sometimes have met in subgroupings in various homes, it seems that on occasion they assembled as an entire community in a single place (14:23). Thus, their number would not have been more than could be accommodated in a first-century Corinthian home. Mansions of the super-elite were immense. But lacking any members from the socioeconomic stratosphere, the largest houses available to the community for its meetings would have been those of moderately wealthy members. Archaeologists' findings suggest that such houses could typically accommodate a gathering of some forty to fifty people. The church community, then, to which Paul wrote may have been smaller than all but the tiniest local Christian congregations today.

Despite their small number, the Christians in Corinth were far from being a harmonious bunch. In fact, stresses and strains in their relationships are the leading problem that Paul deals with in his letter. Among the areas of conflict:

- ◆ Prestige-seeking members, perhaps especially the upper-class men who host the community's gatherings, have brought their competitive style of relating to each other into the Christian community. They are showing off their religious insights and sophisticated speaking abilities—all of which they regard as "wisdom." This is causing the community to contract into rival groups, perhaps meeting in different homes. Paul addresses this situation in the first four chapters of his letter (we read some of this section in Weeks 1 and 2).
- ◆ Members are defrauding each other in business and property transactions and taking each other to court (6:1–11—Week 3).
- ◆ Those who consider themselves more spiritual and better theologically informed engage in disagreements with other members over issues concerning sex and spirituality (chapters 6–7—Week 3) as well as diet and dining (chapters 8–10).
- ◆ Socially advantaged members show no respect for the disadvantaged at celebrations of the Lord's Supper (11:17–34—Week 4).
- ◆ Some members flaunt impressive spiritual gifts in order to raise their social standing, depreciating those with less showy gifts (chapters 12–14—Weeks 5–6).

We can only marvel that such a small group of people could *discover* so many sources of conflict—and that the group could contain so much conflict without bursting apart.

While there is much conflict among the Corinthian Christians, little if any of it concerns Christian teaching. Paul does correct a misunderstanding about the resurrection (15:12). But the Corinthians do not seem to be fighting with each other over this issue or over other doctrinal points. In general, the tensions among the Corinthians lie in the area of Christian living rather than Christian teaching. The Corinthians have brought their pre-Christian outlook into their Christian life. They have not relinquished their city's self-promoting, status-seeking, competitive ethos.

Nor have the Corinthian Christians abandoned the concepts of spirituality that they learned from their Greek cultural environment. Some of them promote a spirituality that scorns the body as unspiritual. This leads some of them to a policy of sexual promiscuity and others to a policy of sexual repression—problems that Paul addresses in chapters 6 and 7. Others embrace an amoral spirituality that feels comfortable combining spiritual experience with jealousy, selfish ambition, dishonesty, litigiousness, sexual promiscuity, frank enjoyment of wealth without concern for the poor, and competitive displays of religiosity. Paul addresses these problems throughout most of his letter.

Paul does not deny that the Corinthians are very spiritual, and *genuinely* spiritual. In becoming Christians, they have received the Holy Spirit, who has brought them an array of gifts, all of which Paul welcomes (1:4–7). But the Corinthians are pouring these authentic experiences and actions of the Spirit into a self-centered mold. The Corinthians have launched themselves into a self-exalting spiritual high (4:8–13). They are treating their spiritual gifts as equipment for social climbing and gaining prestige (chapters 12–14). They are using their spiritual knowledge and eloquence to gain status and outshine rivals (chapters 1–4, 12–14). They disregard the spiritual needs of weaker brothers and sisters (chapters 8–10). They impose an exaggerated asceticism on other people (chapter 7). They embarrass the poor (chapter 11).

Paul calls the Corinthians to leave behind false spiritualities and become truly spiritual. Real spirituality, he insists, is seen most clearly in Jesus' death on the cross. At the cross, we see that real spirituality is, fundamentally, self-giving, because at the cross we see that God is self-giving. Jesus saved us from the power of sin and death by relinquishing his life for us. This kind of love, Paul says, is authentic spirituality in its purest form.

True spirituality, Paul insists, turns all gifts and graces toward the good of others rather than toward the aggrandizement of the self. The truly spiritual person accepts the experiences and workings of the Spirit as aids for advancing God's mission in the world, not for his or her own personal advancement. True spirituality grasps the supremacy of love (chapter 13).

Obviously, the conflict of true and false notions of spirituality was not limited to first-century Greece. Today bookstores and Web sites are crowded with guides to spirituality. Churches and other organizations offer a wide range of spiritual programs. Amid this multitude of spiritualities, the inquirer must seek to distinguish what is genuine from what is false. Which spiritualities lead forward on the journey to the Light that is Love? As a guide to discernment, we could hardly do better than Paul's letter to the Corinthians.

Several themes emerge as Paul leads the Corinthians to deeper conversion in area after area of their community life. One of Paul's themes is that we ourselves and everything we have—our abilities, our knowledge, our bodies, our teachers, our spiritual and material resources—belong entirely to God (3:5–9, 21–23; 6:19–20; 12:4–11). All are gifts. All are to be used for God's purposes. What room does this leave for boasting about ourselves, promoting ourselves, or making a selfish use of anything we have?

A second theme is that as followers of Christ we are brothers and sisters in him. Paul frequently refers to this relationship (1:1, 10, 11; 3:1; 4:6; 5:11; 7:24, 29; 10:1; 12:1; 14:6, 20; 15:1, 50; 16:12, 15, 20. In addition, Paul uses the Greek word for "brother," "brothers," and "sister" in places where the NRSV chooses an alternative translation: 6:6; 7:12; 8:11–13; 9:5; 14:26; 15:58). To treat each other as objects of rivalry or envy, as a means to enlarge our reputation, or as an audience before whom we may display our piety and spirituality—all of this contradicts our relationship in Christ. As brothers and sisters, we should work at understanding *each other's* needs, at devoting our talents and resources to *each other's* welfare. "Do not seek your own advantage," Paul says simply, "but that of the other" (10:24). Do what is upbuilding for others rather than what is simply gratifying for yourself (10:23; 14:4).

A third theme is this: Remember Jesus, crucified and risen from the dead for us (2:2; 11:23–26). If we remember him, we will perceive how we are to live.

A fourth theme is our need to reevaluate ourselves. If anyone thinks he or she is wise, let that person become a fool so as to become truly wise, Paul counsels (see 3:18; 8:2). If we are to advance along the road to God, we must unlearn in order to relearn. The humility to acknowledge our immaturity remains a requirement at every stage of the journey, no matter how long we have been traveling.

These themes offer a great deal for our personal reflection as we ponder our next steps on our life's journey to God. Look for these themes as you read Paul's letter, and reflect on what they mean for you. Paul targets weaknesses and problems in the Corinthians' lives. As we read his letter, we may ask ourselves how we are like them. In what ways do we view the world from a skewed perspective, as they did? To what degree do we share the values and attitudes that Paul urges them to change? Paul wrote to Christians in ancient Corinth; in what way do his words speak to each of us?

At a couple of points in his letter, Paul speaks sharply to the Corinthians about problems in their Christian community. For the most part, however, he patiently reasons with them. Paul regards some of the Corinthians' problems as fairly serious, but he does not seem worried about his new Christian friends (1:8–9). The Holy Spirit is remarkably active among them. Apparently Paul is not surprised that the Spirit would bring to light areas in their lives that need to change. Paul seems to accept Christian life as a lengthy and messy process.

From our own experience, we know that Christian life continues to be a messy process. But the Spirit is as richly present among us today as he was in ancient Corinth. Like our Corinthian ancestors in faith, we can make progress by going back to the beginning, to Jesus crucified and risen. He will always be the beginning, the way, and the end of our journey into Light.

In this Six Weeks guide, we will focus on six portions of Paul's letter that bear especially on the theme of deeper conversion to Christ. In the process, we will skip over sections where Paul speaks about his ministry as an apostle (chapter 4), about a problem of sexual immorality (chapter 5), about questions of marriage and singlehood (chapter 7), about eating meat that may have been offered to pagan gods before being offered for sale in the market (chapters 8–10), about head coverings when the community worships (11:2–16), about the Resurrection (chapter 15), and about his travel plans (chapter 16). You can enhance your appreciation of the excerpts we do read in this guide by reading Paul's entire letter. If you do so, you may find it helpful to use a study Bible, with notes and other helpful materials (see page 80).

Week 1

The Foolishness of God

Questions to Begin

15 minutes
Use a question or two to get warmed up for the reading.

---

1 From whom would you be especially surprised and pleased to receive a letter, e-mail, or phone call today?

---

2 Who is the most effective speaker, religious or not, you have ever heard?

Opening the Bible

5 minutes
Read the passage aloud. Let individuals take turns reading paragraphs.

The Reading: 1 Corinthians 1:1–2:5

Dear Corinthians . . .

1 Paul, called to be an apostle of Christ Jesus by the will of God, and
our brother Sosthenes,

2 To the church of God that is in Corinth, to those who are
sanctified in Christ Jesus, called to be saints, together with all those
who in every place call on the name of our Lord Jesus Christ, both
their Lord and ours:

3 Grace to you and peace from God our Father and the Lord
Jesus Christ.

You're So Gifted!

4 I give thanks to my God always for you because of the grace of God
that has been given you in Christ Jesus, 5 for in every way you have been
enriched in him, in speech and knowledge of every kind—6 just as the
testimony of Christ has been strengthened among you—7 so that you are
not lacking in any spiritual gift as you wait for the revealing of our Lord
Jesus Christ. 8 He will also strengthen you to the end, so that you may be
blameless on the day of our Lord Jesus Christ. 9 God is faithful; by him
you were called into the fellowship of his Son, Jesus Christ our Lord.

So How Come You're Splitting Up into Factions?

10 Now I appeal to you, brothers and sisters, by the name of our Lord
Jesus Christ, that all of you be in agreement and that there be no
divisions among you, but that you be united in the same mind and the
same purpose. 11 For it has been reported to me by Chloe's people that
there are quarrels among you, my brothers and sisters. 12 What I mean
is that each of you says, "I belong to Paul," or "I belong to Apollos,"
or "I belong to Cephas," or "I belong to Christ." 13 Has Christ been
divided? Was Paul crucified for you? Or were you baptized in the name
of Paul? 14 I thank God that I baptized none of you except Crispus and
Gaius, 15 so that no one can say that you were baptized in my name.
16 (I did baptize also the household of Stephanas; beyond that, I do not
know whether I baptized anyone else.) 17 For Christ did not send me to
baptize but to proclaim the gospel, and not with eloquent wisdom, so
that the cross of Christ might not be emptied of its power.

Remember Jesus' Death

18 For the message about the cross is foolishness to those who are
perishing, but to us who are being saved it is the power of God.
19 For it is written,

> "I will destroy the wisdom of the wise,
> and the discernment of the discerning I will thwart."

20 Where is the one who is wise? Where is the scribe? Where is the
debater of this age? Has not God made foolish the wisdom of the
world? 21 For since, in the wisdom of God, the world did not know
God through wisdom, God decided, through the foolishness of our
proclamation, to save those who believe. 22 For Jews demand signs
and Greeks desire wisdom, 23 but we proclaim Christ crucified, a
stumbling block to Jews and foolishness to Gentiles, 24 but to those
who are the called, both Jews and Greeks, Christ the power of God
and the wisdom of God. 25 For God's foolishness is wiser than human
wisdom, and God's weakness is stronger than human strength.

Remember Your Own Situation and My Preaching to You

26 Consider your own call, brothers and sisters: not many of you were
wise by human standards, not many were powerful, not many were of
noble birth. 27 But God chose what is foolish in the world to shame
the wise; God chose what is weak in the world to shame the strong;
28 God chose what is low and despised in the world, things that are
not, to reduce to nothing things that are, 29 so that no one might
boast in the presence of God. 30 He is the source of your life in Christ
Jesus, who became for us wisdom from God, and righteousness and
sanctification and redemption, 31 in order that, as it is written, "Let
the one who boasts, boast in the Lord."

2:1 When I came to you, brothers and sisters, I did not come
proclaiming the mystery of God to you in lofty words or wisdom.
2 For I decided to know nothing among you except Jesus Christ, and
him crucified. 3 And I came to you in weakness and in fear and in
much trembling. 4 My speech and my proclamation were not with
plausible words of wisdom, but with a demonstration of the Spirit
and of power, 5 so that your faith might rest not on human wisdom
but on the power of God.

Questions for Careful Reading

10 minutes
Choose questions according to your interest and time.

---

1 Does Paul express thanks for anything the Corinthians have done (1:4–9)? For whose actions does Paul express thanks?

---

2 Count up the times Paul mentions Jesus in the opening of his letter (1:1–9). How might Paul's handling of the problem of division in 1:10–2:5 account for his numerous references to Jesus at the outset?

---

3 Paul reminds the Corinthians that God has "called" them (1:2). What has God called them to? What resources has God given them for this process?

---

4 In 1:13, why does Paul speak of himself rather than of Apollos or Peter ("Cephas")?

---

5 "Has not God *made foolish* the wisdom of the world?" (1:20—emphasis added). The Greek form of the verb refers to a single act at a particular moment. What particular act might Paul be thinking of?

A Guide to the Reading

If participants have not read this section already, read it aloud. Otherwise go on to "Questions for Application."

1:1–17. Paul begins on a positive note, acknowledging the spiritual knowledge and understanding that God has given the Corinthians (1:4–7). But he quickly moves on to show them that they are not as wise as they think.

The Corinthians are dividing up into cliques aligned with different leaders: Paul, Cephas (that is, Peter; Cephas reflects the Aramaic form of his name), and Apollos (a prominent teacher: Acts 18:24–19:1). What is the Christ faction? Perhaps it is a default group consisting of those who wish their fellow factionalizing brethren would give it a rest ("Can't we all just be Christians?"). There is no evidence in Paul's letter that Peter and Apollos themselves are opposing Paul. Paul and Apollos are still cooperating with each other (16:12). But their followers are creating factions around them.

Paul's language—"be in agreement . . . united in the same mind and the same purpose"—indicates that conflicting opinions are in play. But what are they? The factions do not seem to be based on theological disagreements. Paul gives no indication that some in the community are opposing his teaching while others remain faithful to it—no indication, for example, that while Paul preached Christ crucified, Peter or Apollos did not. Significantly, Paul does not rebuke the Peter or Apollos groups in particular. Indeed, the only ones he singles out for reproach are his own partisans (1:13).

The root problem, it seems, is not rival theologies but rivalry itself. It is not a matter of competing doctrines but of competing egos. One scholar remarks that it is the "I" in the "I belong to" statements that Paul argues against. To declare that "*my* teacher is greater than *your* teacher" is to rank not only the teachers but also *you* and *me.* In Corinth, party spirit seems to have developed almost in pure form, not based on particular beliefs but solely on particular persons' ambitions.

How has this happened? First-century Greek and Roman society was even more inclined than our own to applaud naked self-promotion. Men, especially, competed quite openly for honor and influence. Business, politics, the military, law, medicine, philosophy, religious institutions—all were viewed as arenas where men might legitimately vie for prominence and power. The Christians in Corinth have brought this status-seeking outlook into their lives as Christians. They are playing out their struggle for prestige and influence within the Church, just as they were accustomed to doing in business, professional associations, and civic life. The tone of their ambitious jockeying for honor can be detected in Paul's repeated references to "boasting" (1:29–31; 3:21; 4:7).

In the face of the Corinthians' factionalism, Paul could merely have made an argument regarding effectiveness: "You'll accomplish more if you work as a team." Instead, he leads them to reflect on their life in Christ. He challenges them to consider the glaring contradiction between their outlook and that of Jesus. Paul's goal is to bring them not only to outward harmony but to a deeper conversion to their Lord.

1:18–25. In the Corinthians' status-obsessed culture, most people viewed education and eloquence largely as means to fame and fortune. People used philosophical ideas and polished oratory to advance their careers. This is exactly what the Corinthian Christians are doing. They are treating Christianity as a body of religious knowledge that gives them an opportunity to display their clever insight and oratorical skills. They are using the church as a forum for debating and for networking to advance their social standing. This worldly use of knowledge and communication skills is what Paul means by "eloquent wisdom" (1:17), "wisdom of the world" (1:20), "lofty words or wisdom" (2:1).

The total inadequacy of this worldly wisdom, Paul points out, has been demonstrated by the inability of its followers to perceive the way that God acted through Jesus. People who were locked into worldly wisdom could not see what God was doing through Jesus' death. From a worldly point of view, where one focuses on achieving one's own selfish goals, Jesus' voluntary death appears to be stupid (1:23). People geared towards self-fulfillment and self-aggrandizement simply cannot comprehend a God who loves so much that he would humble himself to save even his enemies (Romans 5:8).

By contrast, the Jewish people did possess genuine wisdom in their Scriptures. Quite reasonably, they looked for "signs" that would help them determine where and how God was accomplishing the plan of salvation foreshadowed in Scripture. Nevertheless, many of them, too, failed to correctly interpret the signs that God gave. They, too, viewed Jesus from a worldly standpoint, from which Jesus' humiliating and painful death hardly looked like a conquest of evil and oppression. They were not open to the wisdom by which God had acted through the death of Jesus.

Paul's point is that God has pulled the rug out from under the worldly-wise outlook. Jesus' offering of his life on the cross was the wisest and most powerful action in history. Through it, God has rescued the human race from the power of sin and the finality of death. The worldly, self-seeking mentality, which regards Jesus' death as weak and foolish, is foolish. Indeed, it is an obstacle to knowing God and understanding how he is at work in the world.

1:26–31. The Corinthians are vying with each other to be perceived as wise and learned, to gain power and influence. It is a good thing God did not operate with your value system, Paul tells them. If God had adopted the Corinthians' valuation of wealth, education, and noble birth, he would have passed by the Corinthians, for few of them were notable in these ways. God, however, values people regardless of their wealth, knowledge, or social standing. He wishes all people to hear and respond to the gospel of his Son. Since most people in the world are relatively poor, God's universal invitation means that most of those he calls are poor. The Corinthians should be the first to appreciate God's system of values, for it has given them a place in his kingdom. Why would they continue to embrace a system of values that would have excluded them from God's kingdom?

If the Corinthians did not receive life in Christ through their wisdom, wealth, or noble birth, but through God's gift, they have no basis for boasting (1:31), for proclaiming their own greatness, for placing themselves over other people, for advertising themselves as theologically insightful or holy.

2:1–5. The Corinthians who are turning the gospel into material for self-promotion should also remember *how* the gospel came to them. Paul did not deliver it with entertaining speeches and clever slogans. He did not arrive in Corinth looking to please audiences and elicit applause, to enlarge his reputation as a speaker and thinker, to get himself invited to dinner in the best homes. Basically, Paul announced what God has done through Jesus' death and resurrection. Paul's concern was not to promote himself as a spiritual guru but to meet God's expectations for his ministry—a concern that had him in "fear" and "trembling."

Paul does not deny that he used reasonable persuasion (2:4; consider Acts 17). But he did not let his rhetoric get in the way of the reality he was attempting to communicate (1:17). Above all, he did not let *himself* get in the way of his message. He wanted Jesus, not Paul, to be the focus of attention. He wanted his listeners' new relationship with God to be founded on what God had done for them through Jesus' saving death, not on the brilliance of the preacher (2:5).

"Clever thinking and clever speech?" Paul says to the Corinthians. "Those don't bring anyone closer to God. The greatest cleverness in the world failed to recognize God's most profound action in the world. By getting wrapped up in your religious arguments, you have gone astray, even if your arguments are correct. Self-promoting displays of religious thinking are not the way to know God. God has revealed himself in an act of total love, humility, and self-giving—the exact opposite of the self-promotion at work in your religious talk. The beginning of real wisdom is to fall silent and contemplate the crucifixion of Jesus. *There* is a wisdom you would never have thought of, no matter how wise you are. If you contemplate *that* wisdom, you will see your ego trips as the foolishness that they are, distracting you from the great thing that God has done. In Jesus' self-giving you will find the inspiration to put aside your status seeking and to serve one another."

Questions for Application

40 minutes
Choose questions according to your interest and time.

---

1 Paul was called by God to be an apostle (1:1). What has God called you to be?

---

2 Wisdom is both a strong point and a weak point for the Corinthians. In what way may a person's strong points also be their points of weakness, temptation, and vulnerability? How can recognizing this be helpful?

---

3 Paul celebrates the Corinthians' gifts (1:7–8) before correcting their problems. How important is it to affirm people's knowledge and abilities in the process of helping them to learn and grow?

---

4 How can a person detect his or her own worldly values? Is it easier to see others' worldly values than your own? (See Matthew 7:1–5.)

---

5 What motivates people to compete with each other? What are the positive and negative aspects of competition? In what ways is competitiveness inappropriate in the Church?

6 Paul indicates that there should be a match between the content of the Christian message and the way it is communicated (1:17 and 2:2–5). How does the way you live and treat other people help them understand the Christian message? How might it be an obstacle to their understanding?

7 For personal reflection: Because he loved them, God chose the members of the church in Corinth even though in the view of society they were "foolish . . . weak . . . low and despised" (1:27–28). Thus he showed what he thinks of human standards of importance. Who do you choose as your friends? Who do you make an effort to get to know? What are your standards for who you will love?

Bible study will have an effect on our lives. It will result in growth, and that means change. . . . If we are not prepared to change in some way, we better not risk studying the Bible.

Rolf E. Aaseng, *A Beginner's Guide to Studying the Bible*

Approach to Prayer

15 minutes
Use this approach—or create your own!

- Let one participant read 1 Corinthians 2:1–2 aloud. Pause for silent reflection. Then pray together this prayer attributed to St. Bernard of Clairvaux. If you know the music by J. S. Bach to which it is often sung, sing it together.

O sacred head surrounded
by crown of piercing thorn,
O bleeding head so wounded,
reviled and put to scorn,
our sins have marred the glory
of thy most holy face,
yet angel hosts adore thee,
and tremble as they gaze.

I see thy strength and vigor
all fading in the strife,
and death with cruel rigor
bereaving thee of life.
O agony and dying!
O love to sinners free!
Jesus, all grace supplying,
O turn thy face on me.

In this thy bitter passion,
Good shepherd, think of
me,
with thy most sweet compassion,
unworthy though I be;
beneath thy cross abiding
forever would I rest,
in thy dear love confiding
and with thy presence
blessed.

A Living Tradition

God's Weakness Triumphs

This section is a supplement for individual reading.

St. John Chrysostom, a fourth-century Greek-speaking bishop, lived in the period when the Roman persecutions of Christians had ceased and Christianity had become the official religion of the Roman Empire. Looking back over the three centuries of persecution, Chrysostom marveled at the way that Christianity, despite repression and killings, had spread from one end of the empire to the other, and beyond.

In this growth, Chrysostom saw an illustration of Paul's words about God's seemingly weak and foolish way of doing things. Jesus' death on the cross might be expected to repel people, Chrysostom pointed out in a homily on 1 Corinthians. When people ask us for a powerful and reasonable sign to confirm our announcement about Jesus, Chrysostom said to his parishioners, not only do we fail to give them what they seek, but we present them with the very opposite. For not only does the cross not seem to be the kind of sign sought by human reason, it is "the annihilation of a sign." Not only is the cross not a display of power, it appears to be convincing evidence of weakness. Consequently, Chrysostom said, "When they who seek for signs and wisdom receive not what they ask for, but the opposite of what they desire—*and then are persuaded,* is not the power of the One who is preached shown to be marvelous? The cross seems to be an obstacle. Nevertheless, not only does it not repel people, it attracts them!"

Chrysostom also expressed amazement at the way that unschooled fishermen and other ordinary folks had succeeded in persuading a whole civilization to change its beliefs and customs. This was more than great philosophers had been able to accomplish. For example, Chrysostom observed, Plato worked hard to show that the soul is immortal, yet he did not persuade many hearers. But the seemingly weak and foolish cross of Christ, working not through religious professionals or skilled communicators but through unlearned men and women, had drawn the whole world to itself, persuading people to change their long-held beliefs about God and about the right way to live. "See how God's foolishness is wiser than human beings and his weakness stronger. While ten thousands were attempting to extinguish the name of the crucified, the opposite came to pass!"

Week 2

We Are Taught by the Spirit

Questions to Begin

15 minutes
Use a question or two to get warmed up for the reading.

1 If you feel comfortable, share some little secret about yourself that no one knows.

2 Describe a possession, large or small, that is particularly important to you.

Opening the Bible

5 minutes
Read the passage aloud. Let individuals take turns reading paragraphs.

The Reading: 1 Corinthians 2:6–3:9, 21–23

True Wisdom Comes from God's Spirit

6 Yet among the mature we do speak wisdom, though it is not a
wisdom of this age or of the rulers of this age, who are doomed to
perish. 7 But we speak God's wisdom, secret and hidden, which God
decreed before the ages for our glory. 8 None of the rulers of this age
understood this; for if they had, they would not have crucified the
Lord of glory. 9 But, as it is written,

"What no eye has seen, nor ear heard,
nor the human heart conceived,
what God has prepared for those who love him"—

10 these things God has revealed to us through the Spirit; for the Spirit
searches everything, even the depths of God. 11 For what human
being knows what is truly human except the human spirit that is
within? So also no one comprehends what is truly God's except the
Spirit of God. 12 Now we have received not the spirit of the world,
but the Spirit that is from God, so that we may understand the gifts
bestowed on us by God. 13 And we speak of these things in words not
taught by human wisdom but taught by the Spirit, interpreting
spiritual things to those who are spiritual.

14 Those who are unspiritual do not receive the gifts of God's
Spirit, for they are foolishness to them, and they are unable to
understand them because they are spiritually discerned. 15 Those who
are spiritual discern all things, and they are themselves subject to no
one else's scrutiny.

16 "For who has known the mind of the Lord
so as to instruct him?"
But we have the mind of Christ.

3:1 And so, brothers and sisters, I could not speak to you as spiritual
people, but rather as people of the flesh, as infants in Christ. 2 I fed
you with milk, not solid food, for you were not ready for solid food.
Even now you are still not ready, 3 for you are still of the flesh. For as
long as there is jealousy and quarreling among you, are you not of the
flesh, and behaving according to human inclinations? 4 For when one
says, "I belong to Paul," and another, "I belong to Apollos," are you
not merely human?

Why Fight over What Belongs to God?

5 What then is Apollos? What is Paul? Servants through whom you
came to believe, as the Lord assigned to each. 6 I planted, Apollos
watered, but God gave the growth. 7 So neither the one who plants
nor the one who waters is anything, but only God who gives the
growth. 8 The one who plants and the one who waters have a common
purpose, and each will receive wages according to the labor of each.
9 For we are God's servants, working together; you are God's field, . . .

21 So let no one boast about human leaders. For all things are
yours, 22 whether Paul or Apollos or Cephas or the world or life or
death or the present or the future—all belong to you, 23 and you
belong to Christ, and Christ belongs to God.

Questions for Careful Reading

10 minutes
Choose questions according to your interest and time.

1 What does Paul mean by "mature" in 2:6?

2 Does the wisdom that God's Spirit gives concern things past, present, or future?

3 Who is included in the "we" in 2:16?

4 If being "of the flesh" gives rise to "jealousy and quarreling" (3:1–3), what would being "spiritual" give rise to?

5 Based on this reading, what does Paul think about how a person can grow in wisdom?

A Guide to the Reading

If participants have not read this section already, read it aloud. Otherwise go on to "Questions for Application."

2:6–3:4. Paul continues to address the problem of factions among the Corinthians. With their jealousy and quarreling, they are "behaving according to human inclinations" (3:3). They are using the church as a forum for their ambitions and rivalry, rallying around prominent leaders in order to enhance their own prestige. They show off how eloquently they can express spiritual ideas, how subtle is their analysis of spiritual issues. Paul has argued that this human "wisdom" in the service of self-advancement is not wisdom at all. Better the "foolishness" of the cross of Christ than wisdom as the Corinthians understand it (1:18–2:5).

Now Paul shifts his line of argumentation. Since the Corinthians are so interested in wisdom, Paul tells them that Christians *do* have a kind of wisdom (2:6). Are they ready and willing to receive it?

Is this wisdom of which Paul now speaks different from the gospel that he has already dealt with (1:18–25)? That cannot be. Paul has declared that Jesus' life-giving death *is* God's wisdom (1:23–25, 30). Nothing can be wiser than that! The deeper we penetrate God's purposes for us, the more clearly we will see Jesus, crucified and risen, at the center. Thus, when Paul now speaks of wisdom, he can mean only some application or extension of the wisdom of the cross.

This wisdom that God gives, Paul says, concerns "what God has prepared for those who love him" (2:9). And it gives us insight not only into what God has prepared for us in his future kingdom but also into what God has prepared for our lives here and now, for it brings understanding of "the gifts bestowed on us by God" (2:12). The Spirit helps us understand the relationship with God that he has granted us already through the crucified Messiah.

Paul says the Corinthians have not been able to receive this wisdom (3:1–2). Does he mean there are two levels of Christians? Does he envision a two-tiered Church, in which the basic gospel is communicated to the immature and mysteries are unfolded for the mature? Hardly. Paul is trying to *overcome* factions in the church, not get new ones started.

There are not two levels of Christians, because true wisdom comes through the Holy Spirit (2:10–11) and *all* Christians have received the Spirit (2:12; 3:16; 6:19; 12:13). Paul's talk about "spiritual people" and "people of flesh" is not a way of dividing the Corinthians into two groups but of highlighting the division within each of their hearts. The Corinthians are spiritual and unspiritual at the same time. They have accepted the gospel, which is true wisdom; they have received the Spirit. Yet they continue to look at life from a limited, worldly point of view—a point of view from which the gospel makes no sense.

The Corinthians are caught in the paradox of not yet being what they already are. They *have* the mind of Christ (2:16)—his outlook, his mental stance—as a gift of the Spirit (1:4–7). But they have not made it their own. They have not put on Jesus' way of thinking. They need to stop acting like people who have not received the Spirit and become the spiritual people they really are. Concretely, they need to leave behind the self-promoting mentality that leads to rivalries and factions, a mentality that is the opposite of love leading to unity.

Those who put Jesus to death did not recognize him as the glorious Lord (2:6, 8). Not only did they not see his heavenly splendor, which was hidden from all human eyes; they did not see the glory of his love, expressed through his voluntary death for the redemption of the world. To see the glory of God's love shining out from Golgotha requires us to reject worldly wisdom and open our minds to the Spirit of God. But the Corinthians have only begun to perceive the glory of their crucified Lord.

3:5–9, 21–23. Paul brings an additional argument to bear against the Corinthian Christians' competitive mentality. Factionalism speaks in the language of *me* and *my: my* opinions, *my* teacher. Yet this assertion of *me* makes no sense in a Church that belongs to God. The leaders around whom the factions are forming in Corinth are nothing in themselves but only agents of God—they are *God's* servants, who will be evaluated and rewarded by *God* (3:8–9). "God's . . . God's . . . God's . . . " Paul intones (3:9). As New Testament scholar Gordon Fee writes, "It is absolutely not permissible to say 'I belong to Paul,' since the only legitimate 'slogan' is 'we all belong to God.'"

Questions for Application

40 minutes
Choose questions according to your interest and time.

1 In what ways was Jesus' death an expression of wisdom? How does this wisdom guide your own life? How would your life be different if you were more deeply shaped by this wisdom?

2 How would you describe Paul's manner of dealing with the Corinthians about their divisions? What could you learn from Paul about dealing with conflicts in your life?

3 What could be learned from Paul about how to deal with conflicts in parishes and Christian organizations? How can Christians distinguish between jealous factionalism, legitimate differences of opinion, and disagreements over fundamental issues of Christian teaching?

4 Do people automatically grow wiser as they grow older? Why or why not?

5 How can we cooperate with the Holy Spirit's attempts to lead us to greater wisdom? How do we sometimes interfere with the Spirit's activity in us?

6 The saints embody the Church's traditions of spirituality. What role do the saints' lives play in your growing in the wisdom that Paul speaks about in this reading? Which saints do you find especially helpful? How could you make greater use of their examples?

7 What situation in your life might you handle better by recognizing that something or someone belongs ultimately to God rather than to you?

8 For personal reflection: How have you experienced the paradox of not yet being what you are already in Christ? How can you cooperate with God's grace to become more the person that you are in Christ?

As seekers, we cannot just skim the surface, amassing bits of unconnected information. Despite promises we often hear, there is no instant wisdom. Genuine wisdom requires the patient process of seeing the connections between facts and relating them to form the bigger picture. Reading for meaning demands that we discover how what we read connects with what we experience. . . . Learning to read the Bible we learn to read our lives at a deeper, spiritual level.

Steve Mueller, *The Seeker's Guide to Reading the Bible*

Approach to Prayer

15 minutes
Use this approach—or create your own!

- Pray for wisdom with these two prayers that call on the Holy Spirit using the imagery of water and of fire. Begin by praying together the first prayer, which comes from the Mass of the Feast of Pentecost:

  May the outpouring of the Holy
  Spirit,
  O Lord, cleanse our hearts and,
  like dew on dry ground,
  make them fruitful.

  Then allow time for members of the group to mention areas of their lives where they seek God's wisdom. Close by praying together the second prayer, drawn from Blessed Columba Marmion, an Irish-born Belgian monk who died in 1923:

  Come, Spirit of Truth,
  and enlighten our minds.
  Set our hearts on fire
  with the same burning love
  that blazes up unceasingly
  in you.

Saints in the Making

What Is That Joy?

This section is a supplement for individual reading.

St. Anselm, an eleventh-century monk, became archbishop of Canterbury, England. In his book *Proslogium* he speculates on the joy of heaven but then wonders whether any conception that his mind is capable of forming could approach the reality of eternal life with God. Here Anselm questions God about his mental picture of heaven:

Tell your servant, Lord, within his heart, if that which I conceive is the joy into which your servants will enter who enter into the joy of their Master (Matthew 25:21, 23). But certainly the joy with which your chosen ones will rejoice "no eye has seen, nor ear heard, nor the human heart conceived" (1 Corinthians 2:9). Therefore, Lord, I have not yet expressed or conceived how much your blessed ones will rejoice. In any case, they will rejoice to the degree that they love, and they will love to the degree that they know. How much, Lord, they will know you then! And how much they will love you! Certainly in this present life "no eye has seen, nor ear heard, nor the human heart conceived" how much they will know and love you in that life.

I pray, God, that I might know you, might love you, in order to rejoice in you. And if I cannot do it fully in this life, may I at least make progress day by day. May knowledge of you grow in me here, and there reach fullness. May your love increase and there become full, so that here my joy might be great in hope and there might be full in reality.

Lord, through your Son you advise us to ask and you promise that we will receive, so that our joy may be full (John 16:24). I do ask, Lord. Let me receive what you promise by your truth, so that my joy may be full. Truthful God, I ask! Let me receive, so that my joy may be full. In the meantime, may my mind meditate on your promise and my tongue speak of it. May my heart love it and my mouth discuss it. May my spirit hunger for it and my flesh thirst for it. May my whole being desire it, until I enter into your joy, my Lord—you who are the Three and One God, blessed for ages. Amen.

Week 3

Litigation? And Prostitution?

Questions to Begin

15 minutes
Use a question or two to get warmed up for the reading.

---

1 What is your favorite book, movie, or TV program involving lawyers?

---

2 What's the most unusual meal you have ever eaten?

Opening the Bible

5 minutes
Read the passage aloud. Let individuals take turns reading paragraphs.

The Reading: 1 Corinthians 6

No Way to Treat Each Other

6:1 When any of you has a grievance against another, do you dare to
take it to court before the unrighteous, instead of taking it before the
saints? 2 Do you not know that the saints will judge the world? And if
the world is to be judged by you, are you incompetent to try trivial
cases? 3 Do you not know that we are to judge angels—to say nothing
of ordinary matters? 4 If you have ordinary cases, then, do you
appoint as judges those who have no standing in the church? 5 I say
this to your shame. Can it be that there is no one among you wise
enough to decide between one believer[a] and another, 6 but a believer[a]
goes to court against a believer[a]—and before unbelievers at that?

7 In fact, to have lawsuits at all with one another is already a
defeat for you. Why not rather be wronged? Why not rather be
defrauded? 8 But you yourselves wrong and defraud—and believers[b]
at that.

9 Do you not know that wrongdoers will not inherit the
kingdom of God? Do not be deceived! Fornicators, idolaters,
adulterers, male prostitutes, sodomites, 10 thieves, the greedy,
drunkards, revilers, robbers—none of these will inherit the kingdom
of God. 11 And this is what some of you used to be. But you were
washed, you were sanctified, you were justified in the name of the
Lord Jesus Christ and in the Spirit of our God.

No Way to Treat Your Bodies

12 "All things are lawful for me," but not all things are beneficial.
"All things are lawful for me," but I will not be dominated by
anything. 13 "Food is meant for the stomach and the stomach for
food,"[c] and God will destroy both one and the other. The body is
meant not for fornication but for the Lord, and the Lord for the body.
14 And God raised the Lord and will also raise us by his power. 15 Do

[a] Greek *brother*
[b] Greek *brothers*
[c] The quotation may extend to the word *other*

you not know that your bodies are members of Christ? Should I
therefore take the members of Christ and make them members of a
prostitute? Never! [16] Do you not know that whoever is united to a
prostitute becomes one body with her? For it is said, "The two shall
be one flesh."

[17] But anyone united to the Lord becomes one spirit with him.
[18] Shun fornication! Every sin that a person commits is outside the
body; but the fornicator sins against the body itself. [19] Or do you not
know that your body is a temple of the Holy Spirit within you, which
you have from God, and that you are not your own? [20] For you were
bought with a price; therefore glorify God in your body.

Questions for Careful Reading

10 minutes
Choose questions according to your interest and time.

---

1 Putting 6:9–11 together with 1:26–28, what picture emerges of the Corinthian Christians' background? How might this picture help to explain the kinds of problems that have developed in the church in Corinth?

---

2 Why does Paul place his reminder about serious sin and the Corinthians' conversion (6:9–11) in between his discussions of property disputes (6:1–8) and sexual immorality (6:12–20)?

---

3 Paul does not unpack his reasoning in 6:16–17. How would you explain the point he is making?

---

4 Identify Paul's questions to the Corinthians in this reading. Why does he ask them so many questions?

A Guide to the Reading

If participants have not read this section already, read it aloud. Otherwise go on to "Questions for Application."

6:1–8. Much here is obscure. Paul's concept that Christians will share in Christ's judgment is surprising (6:2; consider Daniel 7:22; Wisdom 3:8). It is hard to tell what kinds of judges Paul wishes them to appoint. And is he recommending a court or a mediation board?

But Paul's central concern is clear enough. The Greek word translated "believer" in verses 5 and 6 means brother. Christians' lawsuits against each other violate their family relationship in Christ. You are brothers and sisters, Paul insists. Treat each other as such!

New Testament scholar Father Jerome Murphy-O'Connor writes: "The mere existence of disputes which necessitated the intervention of an impartial adjudicator proved that the selfish desire to acquire or retain had displaced the love which should characterize the relationship of believers. Paul was . . . prepared to admit that individuals would need help to work through situations of friction. Such help, however, was to be sought within the community." Our relationships with each other as Christians are necessarily different in today's society. Nevertheless, we shouldn't blithely sue a fellow parishioner.

6:9–11. The kingdom of God comes to us as an inheritance and thus is a gift unearned. Yet there is a requirement to receive the gift: our response to God's grace. Yet it is God's faithfulness that enables us to respond to him (see 1:8–9, and the *Catechism of the Catholic Church,* sections 1852-64, 2351-59).

6:12–20. The Corinthians' argument in favor of prostitution is threefold, as is Paul's answer.

The Corinthians: "All things are lawful" (6:12). This slogan perhaps echoes Paul's teaching, since he teaches that Jesus, not the Mosaic Law, is now at the center of our relationship with God. Many requirements of the Mosaic Law are no longer binding, for example, rules regarding circumcision, diet, and holy days. "And sex," the Corinthians add.

Paul: "You're twisting my words." God's call to live justly and care for one another remains. In fact, Christ calls us to love (Galatians 6:2), and loving behavior is constructive: it "builds up" the individual in wholeness and joy; it strengthens the human community (see 8:1). Sin—for example, sexual immorality—is not "beneficial." To allow ourselves to be dominated by our biological and psychological drives is to fall into a kind of addictive behavior that destroys our personalities and harms other people.

The Corinthians: Since the body is transitory, bodily activities are of no lasting significance (6:13; the assertion that God will destroy both stomach and food seems to be part of the Corinthians' slogan). Since the stomach and, it is implied, the sexual organs, will ultimately perish, eating food and having sex are morally insignificant.

Paul: Although we will die and our bodies will rot away, God will recreate our bodies in the resurrection (6:14). In our risen bodies we will live in union with the Lord (6:13–14—a subject that Paul develops in chapter 15). Thus the body is not a disposable sheath for the soul, a kind of clothing that we wear for a while and then discard. The body is an integral part of us. Therefore, what we do with our bodies is of profound importance.

The Corinthians: Just as for food, so also for sex: the body is designed for whatever satisfies its appetites (see 6:13).

Paul: Eating and having sex are not equally significant. Sexual union joins us intimately with another person (6:16). Thus our sexuality is not a merely biological function; it is a means of giving our whole self to another person, a capacity for deep union with another person. While what we eat has no moral importance one way or the other, who we have sex with is of great moral consequence.

All sins, of course, are "against the body," in the sense of using it for selfish purposes. But sexual sins violate the body in a particular way. Since our sexuality gives us a capacity for a loving, faithful relationship with a spouse, to use this capacity for selfish exploitation violates our bodies in a special way.

Christ has purchased us (6:20). We are like slaves who have passed from one owner to another. Now we are united with him (6:17), filled with his Spirit (6:19). To bring ourselves into deep union with another person apart from Christ's will violates our relationship with Christ. Instead, let us dedicate our whole selves to accomplishing his purposes for us.

Questions for Application

40 minutes
Choose questions according to your interest and time.

---

1 How should Christians express their relationship with one another as brothers and sisters in Christ: helping one another in need, resolving conflicts, visiting the sick, comforting the grieving, other ways? By reflecting on your shared relationship with Christ, what specific change might you be led to make in how you relate to members of your parish?

---

2 Paul would like the Christian community in Corinth to be a place where members find support for working out their conflicts with one another. How does your local Christian community help its members learn to deal with conflicts in their personal lives, families, and parish? How might your Christian community do this more effectively?

---

3 When is it useful for those locked in disagreement to draw in a third party to help them work it out? What have you learned from your experiences with this? What have you learned from acting as a third party to help others work out a problem in their relationship with each other?

4 In addition to the arguments against prostitution that Paul makes in this reading, what other arguments against prostitution could be made?

5 Paul deals specifically with prostitution here. How does his reasoning apply to other kinds of sexual immorality?

6 What situation in your life might you handle differently if you reminded yourself that you belong completely to Christ (6:20)?

It has been the sharing of the Scriptures with others . . . in small faith-sharing groups that has most deeply nurtured my biblical spirituality and made all the formal Bible study meaningful in my life.

Dianne Miller, "Can Bible Study Really Change Your Life?" *New Theology Review*

Approach to Prayer

15 minutes
Use this approach—or create your own!

- Begin by praying the Our Father together. Ask someone to read aloud verses 9–11 and verses 19–20 from this week's reading. Allow a little time for silent reflection. Then pray together the prayer of Cardinal Mercier on the following page. End with a Glory to the Father.

Saints in the Making

A Priceless Secret

This section is a supplement for individual reading.

A reflection and prayer by Cardinal Désiré-Joseph Mercier, an early twentieth-century Belgian archbishop.

I am going to reveal to you the secret of holiness and happiness. Every day for five minutes control your imagination and close your eyes to visible things and your ears to the noises of the world, in order to enter into yourself. Then, in the holiness of your baptized soul—knowing that you are a temple of the Holy Spirit!—speak to the Divine Spirit, saying:

Holy Spirit, soul of my soul,
I adore you.
Enlighten and guide me,
strengthen and comfort me.
Tell me what I need to do.
Give me your commands.
I promise to comply with everything
you wish from me
and to accept everything
you allow to happen to me.
Only let me know your will!

If you do this, your life will flow along happily, serenely, and full of consolation, even in the midst of trials. Grace will be given to you in proportion to each trial, giving you the strength to bear it, and you will arrive at the gate of Paradise. This submission to the Holy Spirit is the secret of holiness.

Week 4

Do This in Remembrance of Me

Questions to Begin

15 minutes
Use a question or two to get warmed up for the reading.

1 What is your earliest childhood—or adult—recollection of being at Mass? How did you come to be there?

2 Describe a social occasion when you felt out of place. Looking back on it, are you glad you were there?

Opening the Bible

5 minutes
Read the passage aloud. Let individuals take turns reading paragraphs.

The Reading: 1 Corinthians 10:16–17; 11:17–34

What It Means to Share the Lord's Supper

16 The cup of blessing that we bless, is it not a sharing in the blood of
Christ? The bread that we break, is it not a sharing in the body of
Christ? 17 Because there is one bread, we who are many are one body,
for we all partake of the one bread. . . .

How the Corinthians Are Celebrating the Lord's Supper

11:17 Now in the following instructions I do not commend you,
because when you come together it is not for the better but for the
worse. 18 For, to begin with, when you come together as a church, I
hear that there are divisions among you; and to some extent I believe
it. 19 Indeed, there have to be factions among you, for only so will it
become clear who among you are genuine. 20 When you come
together, it is not really to eat the Lord's supper. 21 For when the time
comes to eat, each of you goes ahead with your own supper, and one
goes hungry and another becomes drunk. 22 What! Do you not have
homes to eat and drink in? Or do you show contempt for the church
of God and humiliate those who have nothing? What should I say to
you? Should I commend you? In this matter I do not commend you!

What They Should Remember about This Supper

23 For I received from the Lord what I also handed on to you, that the
Lord Jesus on the night when he was betrayed took a loaf of bread,
24 and when he had given thanks, he broke it and said, "This is my
body that is for you. Do this in remembrance of me." 25 In the same
way he took the cup also, after supper, saying, "This cup is the new
covenant in my blood. Do this, as often as you drink it, in
remembrance of me." 26 For as often as you eat this bread and drink
the cup, you proclaim the Lord's death until he comes.

27 Whoever, therefore, eats the bread or drinks the cup of the
Lord in an unworthy manner will be answerable for the body and
blood of the Lord. 28 Examine yourselves, and only then eat of the
bread and drink of the cup. 29 For all who eat and drink without
discerning the body, eat and drink judgment against themselves.
30 For this reason many of you are weak and ill, and some have died.

[31] But if we judged ourselves, we would not be judged. [32] But when
we are judged by the Lord, we are disciplined so that we may not be
condemned along with the world.

How They Should Improve Their Celebration

[33] So then, my brothers and sisters, when you come together to eat,
wait for one another. [34] If you are hungry, eat at home, so that when
you come together, it will not be for your condemnation.

Questions for Careful Reading

10 minutes
Choose questions according to your interest and time.

1 Why does Paul think that the Corinthians' celebration of the Lord's Supper is "not for the better but for the worse" (11:17)?

2 Paul could have moved directly from his rebuke in 11:22 to his instruction in 11:33–34. Why did he include his description of the institution of the Lord's Supper in 11:23–26?

3 In light of the problem that Paul is dealing with (11:21–22), what does he mean by receiving communion "in an unworthy manner" (11:27)?

4 One meaning of Paul's reference to "the body" in 11:29 is supplied by 11:23–24: "The Lord Jesus . . . said, 'This is my body.'" What additional sense of "body" might Paul have in mind in 11:29?

A Guide to the Reading

If participants have not read this section already, read it aloud. Otherwise go on to "Questions for Application."

11:17–22. In Corinth the Christians celebrated the Lord's Supper in the course of an actual meal, possibly in the evening (see Acts 20:7), in the homes of wealthier members. Since a typical dining room could serve only nine or ten people, the gatherings would present the hosts with the problem of how to accommodate the rest of the participants.

Scholars suspect the homeowners were dealing with this situation by serving the wealthy guests in the dining room and relegating the rest to the atrium, the entrance lobby of the house. Since the atrium would be sparsely furnished, the guests there might have to stand. The better food is set before the guests in the dining room; food of inferior quality is served in the atrium. Apparently some of the poorer members of the community have difficulty getting away from their work until later in the evening. The hosts do not wait for them, however, and by the time the latecomers arrive, the food is gone. The wealthy are, in effect, eating their own private meal (11:21).

The wealthier members of the community are used to making a display of their wealth and power. In their arrangements for the Lord's Supper, they have brought their upper-class behavior into the heart of the Christian community.

In an earlier section of the letter, Paul insisted that all who share in the "one bread" become "one body" in Christ (10:16–17). Clearly the Corinthians are not treating each other as members of one body. Whose supper are you eating, Paul asks (11:20–21): the Lord's—or your own?

Paul is concerned less with the wealthier members' gluttony and drunkenness than with their treatment of the poorer members. And his concern for the poor focuses not on their hunger but on their humiliation. Notice that he does not oblige the wealthy to bring more food to pass around (11:34). Presumably the poorer members are not chronically hungry and can afford to miss a meal. But publicly embarrassing them is a serious offense.

11:23–26. Let me remind you what the *Lord's* Supper is, Paul continues. At Jesus' last meal before his death, he gave himself to his disciples in the bread and the cup. His words expressed the purpose of his death the following day: On the cross he would offer his life to God "for" his disciples (11:24), that is, as a sacrifice bringing forgiveness of their sins. In his blood (11:25), that is, by his death, he would create a new relationship—a "new covenant"—between them and God.

Jesus established this meal as a "remembrance" of him (11:25). But if the Corinthians were truly remembering Jesus, they would not be treating each other as they are. In his Last Supper, Jesus gave himself totally to his disciples; and on the cross, he gave himself totally for them. Yet, rather than proclaiming their Lord's self-giving death (11:26), the Corinthians' way of celebrating the meal proclaims their class-consciousness and arrogance. The Corinthians' failure to treat each other respectfully makes their meal more a forgetting of their Lord than a remembering of him.

Remembering the Lord's final meal is meant to renew believers' participation in the covenant with God that Jesus has established by his death. This covenant binds the participants in a relationship not only with God but also with one another (10:16–17). By humiliating the poor members at the Lord's Supper, the wealthy violate the very covenant that the meal commemorates and renews.

11:27–32. In one sense, then, the Corinthians are not really celebrating the Lord's Supper ("When you come together, it is not really to eat the Lord's Supper," Paul literally tells them in 11:20). In another sense, however, they are indeed celebrating the Lord's Supper. The Lord is truly present in their celebration. The cup from which they drink *is* "the cup of the Lord" (11:27); they *are* sharing in his body and blood (10:16–17). This is no ordinary banquet! Thus, their mistreatment of one another is not mere rudeness. It is irreverence bordering on sacrilege. By humiliating the poorer members of the Lord's community, the wealthy are despising God's Church (11:22). They are abusing the Lord himself. This is a *very* serious matter, Paul insists.

11:33–34. Paul does not require the wealthy to share their more expensive food with the poorer members. It is not his pastoral policy to expect everyone to live at the same social and economic level (although see 2 Corinthians 8:13–15). But, he insists, social and economic differences should not cause embarrassment to anyone in Christ's Church.

Questions for Application

40 minutes
Choose questions according to your interest and time.

---

1 How well does your local faith community welcome strangers? What could you do to make the community more welcoming?

---

2 In giving assistance to someone, how important is it to help the person maintain his or her dignity? What are ways of helping people that express respect? that are not respectful? Share something you have learned from your own experience about giving or receiving assistance in a way that did—or did not—express respect. What have you learned from this experience?

---

3 In addition to material deprivation, what other kinds of poverty do people suffer today? What kinds of poverty are experienced by members of your local faith community? How do these various forms of poverty prevent people from playing a full role in society? in your parish? How can these barriers be overcome?

4 What range of people does your parish and/or Christian group tend to attract? What might you do to draw in a wider variety of people?

5 What is the connection between recognizing Jesus' presence in the eucharistic bread and cup and recognizing his presence in the community that celebrates the Eucharist?

6 In the century after Paul, Christian communities began to celebrate the Eucharist apart from the serving of an actual meal. Do you think this was a positive development?

I am more and more convinced that, valuable as personal study and prayer from the Bible is, the Word is most powerful when it is being shared among God's people. Our comments and interactions have been immensely enriching to each other through the years.

Kitty Rodgers, "Can Bible Study Really Change Your Life?" *New Theology Review*

Approach to Prayer

15 minutes
Use one of these approaches—or create your own!

- Pray Psalm 81. Let one participant pray the psalm aloud, pausing after each verse. Between verses, let the other participants pray the refrain from Psalm 136: "for his steadfast love endures forever." End with a Glory to the Father.

- Pray Psalm 95. If participants have different translations, take turns reading the verses. Pray the entire psalm together. Pause for silent reflection. Then pray verses 1–7 again. End with a Glory to the Father.

A Living Tradition

As Often As You Eat This Bread

This section is a supplement for individual reading.

Concerning the Lord's Supper, Paul told the Corinthians: "As often as you eat this bread and drink the cup, you proclaim the Lord's death until he comes" (11:26). Little is known about precisely how Christians of the first-century celebrated the Lord's Supper (or, as we commonly call it today, the Eucharist, from the Greek word for "thanks" used in 11:24). Thus we do not know exactly *how* they proclaimed the Lord's death in their celebration. We do know, however, that as the Eucharist developed in the Church over the centuries, it maintained its focus on Jesus' death and resurrection.

In the Eucharist today we proclaim Jesus' death most obviously and simply in the community's acclamation after "the words of institution." When the priest has repeated the words that Jesus spoke at the Last Supper—"this is my body . . . this is my blood . . . "—the entire congregation declares its faith in God's saving action through Jesus by one of three responses: "When we eat this bread and drink this cup, we declare your death, Lord Jesus, until you come in glory." "Christ has died. Christ is risen. Christ will come again." "Dying you destroyed our death. Rising you restored our life. Lord Jesus, come in glory."

This acclamation punctuates the eucharistic prayer, which itself is essentially a lengthy prayer of praise to God, thanking him for his mercy to us, and above all, for his mercy shown in the death and resurrection of his Son. (The eucharistic prayer is the prayer of offering recited by the priest, beginning after the exchange between priest and people "Lift up your hearts. We lift them up to the Lord. . . ." and ending with ". . . all glory and honor is yours, almighty Father, forever and ever. Amen.")

In other ways also we proclaim Jesus' death in the Mass. We express our faith in Jesus' death and resurrection for us, on Sundays and holy days, by reciting the creed. We express this faith by receiving communion. The crucifix (one is present at every eucharistic celebration) gives visual expression to our faith in Jesus' saving death. And finally, we proclaim Jesus' death and resurrection by the way we live after we have completed our liturgical celebration.

Week 5

The Purpose of Your Gifts

Questions to Begin

15 minutes
Use a question or two to get warmed up for the reading.

---

1. When have you used a tool or piece of equipment to do something for which it was not designed? What happened?

---

2. Describe a gift or ability of yours that you think is particularly useful.

Opening the Bible

5 minutes
Read the passage aloud. Let individuals take turns reading paragraphs.

The Reading: 1 Corinthians 12:4–31; 14:1–12

Many Gifts, One Giver

4 Now there are varieties of gifts, but the same Spirit; 5 and there are
varieties of services, but the same Lord; 6 and there are varieties of
activities, but it is the same God who activates all of them in
everyone. 7 To each is given the manifestation of the Spirit for the
common good. 8 To one is given through the Spirit the utterance of
wisdom, and to another the utterance of knowledge according to the
same Spirit, 9 to another faith by the same Spirit, to another gifts of
healing by the one Spirit, 10 to another the working of miracles, to
another prophecy, to another the discernment of spirits, to another
various kinds of tongues, to another the interpretation of tongues.
11 All these are activated by one and the same Spirit, who allots to
each one individually just as the Spirit chooses.

Many Gifted Persons, Members of One Body

12 For just as the body is one and has many members, and all the members of the body, though many, are one body, so it is with Christ. . . .

14 Indeed, the body does not consist of one member but of
many. . . . 16 And if the ear would say, "Because I am not an eye, I do
not belong to the body," that would not make it any less a part of the
body. 17 If the whole body were an eye, where would the hearing be?
If the whole body were hearing, where would the sense of smell be?
18 But as it is, God arranged the members in the body, each one of
them, as he chose. 19 If all were a single member, where would the
body be? 20 As it is, there are many members, yet one body.

21 The eye cannot say to the hand, "I have no need of you,"
nor again the head to the feet, "I have no need of you." 22 On the
contrary, the members of the body that seem to be weaker are
indispensable, 23 and those members of the body that we think less
honorable we clothe with greater honor, and our less respectable
members are treated with greater respect; 24 whereas our more
respectable members do not need this. But God has so arranged the
body, giving the greater honor to the inferior member, 25 that there
may be no dissension within the body, but the members may have the

same care for one another. 26 If one member suffers, all suffer together
with it; if one member is honored, all rejoice together with it.

Various Gifts, One Basic Principle for Using Them

27 Now you are the body of Christ and individually members of it.
28 And God has appointed in the church first apostles, second
prophets, third teachers; then deeds of power, then gifts of healing,
forms of assistance, forms of leadership, various kinds of tongues.
29 Are all apostles? Are all prophets? Are all teachers? Do all work
miracles? 30 Do all possess gifts of healing? Do all speak in tongues?
Do all interpret? 31 But strive for the greater gifts. . . .

14:1 . . . especially that you may prophesy. 2 For those who
speak in a tongue do not speak to other people but to God; for
nobody understands them, since they are speaking mysteries in the
Spirit. 3 On the other hand, those who prophesy speak to other
people for their upbuilding and encouragement and consolation.
4 Those who speak in a tongue build up themselves, but those who
prophesy build up the church. 5 Now I would like all of you to speak
in tongues, but even more to prophesy. One who prophesies is greater
than one who speaks in tongues, unless someone interprets, so that
the church may be built up.

6 Now, brothers and sisters, if I come to you speaking in
tongues, how will I benefit you unless I speak to you in some
revelation or knowledge or prophecy or teaching? 7 It is the same way
with lifeless instruments that produce sound, such as the flute or the
harp. If they do not give distinct notes, how will anyone know what is
being played? 8 And if the bugle gives an indistinct sound, who will
get ready for battle? 9 So with yourselves; if in a tongue you utter
speech that is not intelligible, how will anyone know what is being
said? For you will be speaking into the air. 10 There are doubtless
many different kinds of sounds in the world, and nothing is without
sound. 11 If then I do not know the meaning of a sound, I will be a
foreigner to the speaker and the speaker a foreigner to me. 12 So with
yourselves; since you are eager for spiritual gifts, strive to excel in
them for building up the church.

Questions for Careful Reading

10 minutes
Choose questions according to your interest and time.

1 From the instructions that Paul gives here, what kinds of problems would you suppose have developed among the Christians in Corinth?

2 How would you characterize the tone of Paul's instructions in this reading? Does he seem upset with the Corinthians?

3 Does Paul wish the Corinthians paid less attention to their spiritual gifts?

4 Notice how often Paul uses the word "same" in 12:4–11. How does this repetition underline his key point? What *is* his key point in these verses?

5 From this reading and our earlier readings, what portrait would you paint of the Corinthian Christians' attitudes and relationships with each other?

A Guide to the Reading

If participants have not read this section already, read it aloud. Otherwise go on to "Questions for Application."

12:4–31. Paul discusses spiritual gifts without providing a complete classification. His two lists (12:8–10 and 28–30) are somewhat different. Neither is an exhaustive catalog of the workings of the Spirit.

Paul mentions gifts spanning the range from the remarkable to the almost invisibly ordinary. The gift of "faith" here (12:9) cannot be the same as the faith by which *all* Christians enter life with Christ. Gordon Fee surmises that *faith* here "refers to a supernatural conviction that God will reveal his power or mercy in a special way in a specific instance" (compare 13:2). At the mundane end of the spectrum are "forms of assistance" (12:28)—possibly different kinds of administrative support. In any case, Paul is less concerned with defining the gifts than with communicating a basic attitude toward them.

Paul appreciates the Corinthians' gifts (1:4–7) but criticizes the way they are relating to them. Members who exercise more spectacular gifts are acting self-important (12:21). Those with more "ordinary" gifts are made to feel useless (12:15–16).

In response, Paul proclaims to the Corinthians: You belong to one another! You are parts of one another! Against their individualistic approach, he champions interdependence. God's gifts to us are not tools for making ourselves admired and loved. Coming from one and the same Spirit, all the various gifts are to be used for one purpose: the "common good" (12:7).

God's gifts do not provide any basis for pride. New Testament scholar F. F. Bruce writes that although "some gifts may be more extraordinary and spectacular than others, . . . it does not follow . . . that those who receive them are more spiritual than others," since it is "the same God who activates all of them in everyone" (12:6). Differences in gifts are God's doing (12:18). Another scholar, Anthony Thiselton, writes: "To try to rank some gifts as 'more essential' than others, let alone as marks of advanced status . . . is to offer a blasphemous challenge to God's freedom to choose whatever is his good will for his people. . . . How dare anyone . . . devalue other people's gifts, as if God had not chosen them for the other?"

Without compassion (see 12:26) and teamwork, Paul counsels the Corinthians, their Christian community will be unable to carry out its mission in the world (12:17, 19).

14:1–12. Paul now moves from general principles to a particular case, involving the gifts of "tongues" and "prophecy."

We might wish that Paul had described these two gifts more fully. The gift of tongues here is apparently not a miraculous ability to communicate with people in other languages, since it is used within the church's gathering, not in public—not in the marketplace, for example (14:23, 26–27). Thus this gift does not seem to be the same as that which produced the communications miracle on the first Pentecost (Acts 2:4–13). On the basis of Romans 8:26–27, some scholars suggest that speaking in tongues here is a kind of Spirit-activated language of the unconscious through which the one praying unburdens his or her anxieties and sorrows to God and praises God's literally unspeakable greatness. Prophecy is a gift of the Spirit that brings insight, challenge, comfort, and direction to individuals and the community.

Whatever the exact nature of these two gifts, they are clearly opposites in several ways. Speaking in tongues is unintelligible, prophecy is intelligible; the first is addressed to God, the second to other people; the first benefits the speaker, the second benefits others.

Paul welcomes the gift of tongues (14:5, 18) as well as prophecy. But the principle that gifts should be used to benefit others helps to determine when and where the two gifts are appropriate. Paul argues that since the gift of tongues is helpful only to the speaker, it is appropriate for private prayer but not in an assembly. The gift of tongues might give the speaker a feeling of release and closeness to God, but that is not a benefit to anyone else. Paul opposes getting carried away with one's own spiritual experience in a way that disregards other people's needs. Instead, when the community comes together, those who have a prophetic gift should use it to encourage the other members.

This particular case illustrates a general principle: use your gifts to benefit others rather than yourself (14:12)—a simple principle that is certainly not hard to understand, although it is difficult to practice consistently!

Questions for Application

40 minutes
Choose questions according to your interest and time.

---

1 What gifts and forms of serving are highly regarded in your local faith community? Which gifts are given little recognition? Are gifts for serving in the world rated as highly as those for serving within the Church? From this week's reading, what do you think Paul might say about this valuing of gifts?

---

2 If St. Paul came to visit your parish, what issues concerning the use—or lack of use—of gifts might he comment on?

---

3 What gifts has God given you for contributing to the Church's mission in the world? How are you putting your gifts at the service of others? What training or experience do you need in order to further develop your gifts?

4 How can Christians help each other identify and develop the gifts that God is giving them? How might your local faith community do this more effectively?

5 How might some of the points in Paul's discussion in this reading have implications for how you participate in the Mass?

6 For personal reflection: Do you ever feel that your parish would be better off if certain persons decided to worship elsewhere on Sunday morning, resigned from the parish council, decided to stop teaching in the religious education program, or whatever? How should 12:12–27 affect your thinking?

It is important to concentrate on what we understand and not waste time worrying if, in some biblical expressions, we find it difficult to hear the voice of Christ.

The Taizé Community, *Listening with the Heart*

Approach to Prayer

15 minutes
Use this approach—or create your own!

- To begin, pray the Our Father together. Then mention very briefly the needs of individuals, organizations, and institutions in the Church who are in special need of God's help. Close by praying together this prayer from the Ambrosian Liturgy (the ancient Catholic rite followed by the diocese of Milan, Italy).

  O God,
  the fire of your love
  moved you to send the Holy
  Spirit,
  the Counselor,
  to your disciples.
  Make it possible for your people
  to remain always in your love—
  firm in faith,
  effective in action,
  attentively protecting the unity
  of love.

A Living Tradition

Gifts for All

This section is a supplement for individual reading.

When Catholic bishops from around the world gathered in Vatican Council II (1962–65) to reflect on the nature and mission of the Church, the question arose as to whether the gifts of the Spirit that Paul mentions in 1 Corinthians 12 continue to be present in the Church. Many theologians took the view that these gifts, or "charisms," were given to the early Church to meet its special needs but had long ago died out. Some felt this was for the best, for if laypeople received charisms directly from the Holy Spirit, they would be empowered to act on their own initiative, without waiting for the direction of the bishops, a situation that some feared could lead to anarchy.

In his recollections of the Vatican Council, Cardinal Léon Joseph Suenens of Belgium writes that the mention of the charisms in a draft document under debate "provoked a reaction from Cardinal Ruffini, who asked that this allusion be suppressed, considering that the charisms undoubtedly belonged to the early Church but that mentioning them as still present could provide an opportunity for abuses. It seemed to me, on the contrary, that it was necessary to acknowledge their place and that the charisms of the Holy Spirit constitute an integral part of Christian life and evangelization."

Cardinal Suenens insisted that the Holy Spirit "is not given to pastors only but to each and every Christian." Every Christian, he said, has his or her charism, his or her gift from the Holy Spirit for playing an active role in Christ's work in the world.

The bishops agreed with Cardinal Suenens. In their final statement, they wrote that the Holy Spirit, "allotting his gifts according as he wills (compare 1 Corinthians 12:11) . . . also distributes special graces among the faithful of every rank. By these gifts he makes them fit and ready to undertake various tasks and offices for the renewal and building up of the Church, as it is written, 'the manifestation of the Spirit is given to everyone for profit'(1 Corinthians 12:7). Whether these charisms are very remarkable or more simple and widely diffused, they are to be received with thanksgiving and consolation since they are fitting and useful for the needs of the Church" ("Dogmatic Constitution on the Church," section 12).

Week 6

Love Has the Last Word

Questions to Begin

15 minutes
Use a question or two to get warmed up for the reading.

---

1 Who had the last word in discussions in your family when you were growing up. Who has it now?

---

2 What was the noisiest place you ever lived or worked?

Opening the Bible

5 minutes
Read the passage aloud. Let individuals take turns reading paragraphs.

The Reading: 1 Corinthians 13; Matthew 6:1–4; 18:21–22

How Crucial Love Is!

1 If I speak in the tongues of mortals and of angels, but do not have
love, I am a noisy gong or a clanging cymbal. 2 And if I have
prophetic powers, and understand all mysteries and all knowledge,
and if I have all faith, so as to remove mountains, but do not have
love, I am nothing. 3 If I give away all my possessions, and if I hand
over my body so that I may boast, but do not have love, I gain
nothing.

The Marks of True Love

4 Love is patient; love is kind; love is not envious or boastful or
arrogant 5 or rude. It does not insist on its own way; it is not irritable
or resentful; 6 it does not rejoice in wrongdoing, but rejoices in the
truth. 7 It bears all things, believes all things, hopes all things, endures
all things.

Love Lasts Forever

8 Love never ends. But as for prophecies, they will come to an end; as
for tongues, they will cease; as for knowledge, it will come to an end.
9 For we know only in part, and we prophesy only in part; 10 but
when the complete comes, the partial will come to an end. 11 When I
was a child, I spoke like a child, I thought like a child, I reasoned like
a child; when I became an adult, I put an end to childish ways. 12 For
now we see in a mirror, dimly, but then we will see face to face. Now
I know only in part; then I will know fully, even as I have been fully
known. 13 And now faith, hope, and love abide, these three; and the
greatest of these is love.

Two Sayings of Jesus

Matthew 6:1 "Beware of practicing your piety before others in order to
be seen by them; for then you have no reward from your Father in
heaven. 2 So whenever you give alms, do not sound a trumpet before
you, as the hypocrites do in the synagogues and in the streets, so that
they may be praised by others. Truly I tell you, they have received

their reward. 3 But when you give alms, do not let your left hand
know what your right hand is doing, 4 so that your alms may be done
in secret; and your Father who sees in secret will reward you."

18:21 Then Peter came and said to him, "Lord, if another
member of the church sins against me, how often should I forgive? As
many as seven times?" 22 Jesus said to him, "Not seven times, but, I
tell you, seventy-seven times."

Questions for Careful Reading

10 minutes
Choose questions according to your interest and time.

1 In 13:1, what's wrong with gongs and cymbals? Why are they an apt image for the point that Paul is making?

2 In 13:1–2 Paul mentions gifts about which he wrote in chapter 12—tongues, prophecy, faith. Does giving away one's possessions or handing over one's body as a martyr (13:3) correspond to any of the gifts that Paul spoke about in chapter 12? In what way are these actions gifts?

3 Judging from Paul's corrections of the Corinthians in earlier chapters, in what ways are the Corinthians lacking in the love that he describes in this reading? In what ways is love an essential part of the remedy for the shortcomings in their lives that Paul has pointed out?

4 Drawing from Paul's statements earlier in the letter, what other qualities might be added to his description of love in 13:4–7?

5 In the way Paul has been relating to the Corinthians in this letter, has he practiced what he preaches in 13:4–7?

A Guide to the Reading

If participants have not read this section already, read it aloud. Otherwise go on to "Questions for Application."

If we were to read Paul's recommendation of love by itself, we might conclude that he views love and spiritual gifts as opposite, alternative ways of approaching the Christian life. But Paul does not view spiritual gifts and love as an either-or. This passage on love (chapter 13) lies in the middle of his teaching about how to exercise the spiritual gifts (chapters 12 and 14). Paul is trying to *guide* the use of the gifts of the Spirit, not replace them. His purpose is to lead the Corinthians to use their gifts for other people's benefit rather than for their own. Since it is love that considers other people's needs and tries to meet them, the unspoken word in his instruction on spiritual gifts in chapters 12 and 14 has been *love.* In chapter 13, he speaks the word. Paul views the whole range of gifts of the Spirit as indispensable (12:17, 19, 22), and he views love as the indispensable ingredient in their use. Used with love, our gifts build up the Christian community and extend its mission in the world.

13:1–3. Paul is not here criticizing the gift of tongues (14:5, 18). It is not the gift of tongues that is empty noise, but the person who prays in tongues without love. As to prophetic powers and knowledge, Paul himself abounds in such gifts (2:6–7, 13; 15:51–52). But, he says, if I know what God is about in the world, and even participate in accomplishing his purposes but do not love, I am nothing. Using God's gifts without dedication to others' welfare is an abuse, a failure to appropriate "the mind of Christ" (2:16), who laid down his life for us.

It might seem that giving all our possessions to feed the hungry would necessarily be an expression of love. But Paul asserts that even actions that contribute to others' welfare may lack love. Jesus made the same point. He pointed out that it is possible to act in a loving way from a desire to gain a reputation for being a loving person rather than from a genuine concern for our neighbor. Jesus offered a way to discern our motivation: Do we parade our good deeds openly or keep them secret (Matthew 6:1–4)? Deeds of true love are content to have God as their only audience.

13:4–7. Love is "patient"—the Greek might be translated, "long-tempered." Love has a very long fuse.

Love is not envious, boastful, or arrogant; that is, it is not concerned about gaining social position or compliments. It does not assert that "I am better than you." Love cares for the welfare of others, rather than seeking to advance itself at others' expense. This was the problem among the Corinthians that Paul addressed when he wrote about their ambitiousness and factions (1:10–3:23). Love is not "rude," in other words, it does not behave disgracefully—as the wealthy Corinthians are doing by humiliating the poor at the celebration of the Lord's Supper (11:17–34).

Another possible rendering of 13:7 is: "There is nothing love cannot face; there is no limit to its faith, its hope, its endurance" (Revised English Bible). There is no situation that makes love stop loving. Paul might have added, "love forgives all things," for it is implied in his understanding of love (consider Jesus' instruction about forgiving "seventy-seven times"—Matthew 18:21–22).

13:8–13. "Love never ends" in the sense that nothing that other people do can ever make the one who loves stop desiring what is good for them (13:8). Love "never ends" in another sense too. When everything in this world passes away, and we see God face-to-face, love alone will remain. Love will be the essence of our final relationship with God. Again, Paul is not setting love and spiritual gifts in opposition. He does not say that we should concentrate on loving and forget spiritual gifts. Rather, he states that love, which is the manner in which we should use God's gifts, will outlast all the gifts we use.

Our present "knowledge" of God will ultimately pass away (13:8). In another sense, however, our knowledge will continue and come to completion (13:12). In God's kingdom, our fragmentary knowledge of him in earthly life will give way to a total knowledge. We will leave the marvelous gifts of this world behind us, like children leaving their tricycles on the sidewalk at the end of an afternoon, and we will walk into our Father's house, to enjoy a truly adult relationship with him forever.

Questions for Application

40 minutes
Choose questions according to your interest and time.

---

1 In your experience, who has been an example of the kind of love that Paul describes? What have you learned from this person? What more can you learn from them?

---

2 What situation has been especially important for your learning what it means to love? How has this insight shaped your life?

---

3 What experience has helped you understand the truth of Paul's words in 13:1–3?

---

4 Identify an aspect of Paul's description of love that is difficult for you to put into practice. Who in your life would be most surprised if you were suddenly to do so? (Why not surprise them?)

5 Paul targets the problem of doing good things for selfish reasons (13:3). What difference do the helper's motives make to the person who is helped? Is it possible to have entirely pure motives for doing good? How can a person grow by acting out of genuine love?

6 What is the usefulness of the kind of description of love that Paul gives in 1 Corinthians 13?

7 For personal reflection: What is God's message to you in this week's reading? What step could you take to respond?

To live amidst these things, to meditate on these things, to know nothing else, to seek nothing else, does it not seem to you already here below a foretaste of the heavenly kingdom?

St. Jerome on reading the Bible

Approach to Prayer

15 minutes
Use this approach—or create your own!

- Pray Psalm 84 or 85 together. If participants have different translations, take turns reading the verses. End with an Our Father.

6

1 Corinthians 13; Matthew 6:1–4; 18:21–22

A Living Tradition

Union with God

This section is a supplement for individual reading.

A few comments by St. Thomas Aquinas, the great thirteenth-century theologian, on 1 Corinthians 13.

13:1. God is the life of the soul (". . . he is thy life, . . ."—Deuteronomy 30:20, Douay Version), and the soul that lives by God lives by love ("We know that we have passed from death to life because we love one another. Whoever does not love abides in death"—1 John 3:14). Paul is right, then, to compare speech that lacks love to the sound of dead things, such as brass instruments or cymbals, for although these may make loud noises, yet they are not living, but dead, and dead also is the speech of those who lack love, however eloquent they may be. . . .

13:12. In this present life, we know the invisible God by means of created beings ("Ever since the creation of the world his eternal power and divine nature, invisible though they are, have been understood and seen through the things he has made"—Romans 1:20). Thus the entire creation is a kind of mirror for us because, from the order, goodness, and greatness that God causes in things we come to know the divine wisdom, goodness, and excellence—and this is like seeing in a mirror. . . .

"Now," in this present life, "I know only in part," that is, obscurely and incompletely. "Then," however, that is, in my homeland, "I will know fully, even as I have been fully known." As God knows my essence, so I will know God in his essence—although "as" here means a similarity, not an equality, of knowledge. . . .

13:13. "Now faith, hope, and love abide." The reason he does not mention all the gifts, but only these three, is that these three gifts unite us with God, while the other gifts cannot unite us to God unless they operate through these three. . . .

Because nothing can be loved unless it is known, knowledge of God is required if we are to love him. And because knowing God is beyond our nature, faith is required if we are to know him, for faith grasps things not seen. Then, so that we may not fail or go astray, hope is required, so that we may keep going toward that Goal, confident that it belongs to us. . . . Therefore, these three now remain, but love is greater than all.

Suggestions for Bible Discussion Groups

Like a camping trip, a Bible discussion group works best if you agree on where you're going and how you intend to get there. Many groups use their first meeting to talk over such questions and reach a consensus. Here is a checklist of issues, with bits of advice from people who have experience in Bible discussions. (A planning discussion will go more smoothly if the leaders have thought through the following issues beforehand.)

Agree on your purpose. Are you getting together to gain wisdom and direction for your lives? to finally get acquainted with the Bible? to support one another in following Christ? to encourage those who are exploring—or reexploring—the Church? for other reasons?

Agree on attitudes. For example: "We're all beginners here." "We're here to help one another understand and respond to God's word." "We're not here to offer counseling or direction to one another." "We want to read Scripture prayerfully." What do *you* wish to emphasize? Make it explicit!

Agree on ground rules. Barbara J. Fleischer, in her useful book *Facilitating for Growth,* recommends that a group clearly state its approach to the following:

- *Preparation.* Do we agree to read the material and prepare answers to the questions before each meeting?
- *Attendance.* What kind of priority will we give to our meetings?
- *Self-revelation.* Are we willing to help the others in the group gradually get to know us—our weaknesses as well as our strengths, our needs as well as our gifts?
- *Listening.* Will we commit ourselves to listening to one another?
- *Confidentiality.* Will we keep everything that is shared *with* the group *in* the group?
- *Discretion.* Will we refrain from sharing about the faults and sins of people who are not in the group?
- *Encouragement and support.* Will we give as well as receive?
- *Participation.* Will we give each person the time and opportunity to make a contribution?

You could probably take a pen and draw a circle around *listening* and *confidentiality.* Those two points are especially important.

The following items could be added to Fleischer's list:

- *Relationship with parish.* Is our group part of the adult faith-formation program? independent but operating with the express approval of the pastor? not a parish-based group?
- *New members.* Will we let new members join us once we have begun the six weeks of discussions?

Agree on housekeeping.

- *When will we meet?*
- *How often will we meet?* Meeting weekly or every other week is best if you can manage it. William Riley remarks, "Meetings once a month are too distant from each other for the threads of the last session not to be lost" *(The Bible Study Group: An Owner's Manual).*
- *How long will meetings run?*
- *Where will we meet?*
- *Is any setup needed?* Christine Dodd writes that "the problem with meeting in a place like a church hall is that it can be very soul-destroying," given the cold, impersonal feel of many church facilities. If you have to meet in a church facility, Dodd recommends doing something to make the area homey *(Making Scripture Work).*
- *Who will host the meetings?* Leaders and hosts are not necessarily the same people.
- *Will we have refreshments?* Who will provide them?
- *What about child care?* Most experienced leaders of Bible discussion groups discourage bringing infants or other children to adult Bible discussions.

Agree on leadership. You need someone to facilitate—to keep the discussion on track, to see that everyone has a chance to speak, to help the group stay on schedule. Rena Duff, editor of the newsletter *Sharing God's Word Today,* recommends having two or three people take turns leading the discussions.

It's okay if the leader is not an expert on the Bible. You have this booklet, and if questions come up that no one can answer, you can delegate a participant to do a little research between meetings. It's important for the leader to set an example of listening, to draw out the quieter members (and occasionally restrain the more vocal ones), to move the group on when it gets stuck, to remind the members of their agreements, and to summarize what the group is accomplishing.

Bible discussion is an opportunity to experience the fulfillment of Jesus' promise "Where two or three are gathered in my name, I am there among them" (Matthew 18:20). Put your discussion group in Jesus' hands. Pray for the guidance of the Spirit. And have a great time exploring God's word together!